Harrison, Virginia
The World of Lizards

Where Animals Live

The World of Lizards

Words by Virginia Harrison

Adapted from Mike Linley's
The Lizard in the Jungle

Photographs by
Oxford Scientific Films

Gareth Stevens Children's Books
MILWAUKEE

Contents

Note: The use of a capital letter for a lizard's name means that it is a *species* of lizard (for example, Komodo Dragon). The use of a lower case, or small, letter means that it is member of a larger *group* of lizards.

Lizards in the Jungle

Lizards are cold-blooded *reptiles,* which means
they cannot produce their own body heat as
mammals and birds do. They must warm
themselves in the sun each day. Therefore,
most lizards are found in warm-weather regions.

Five of the 16 main groups of lizard are found in
the *tropical* forest or jungle regions of the world.

The iguanas are medium and large lizards that
live in trees (left). They are *herbivorous,* living
on plants only. The geckoes are insect-eating,
nocturnal, usually small lizards. Chameleons
can change color to match their surroundings,
and catch insects with their long, sticky
tongues. The agamas are *insectivorous* —
they eat only insects — and they are similar to
iguanas. The skinks look like snakes with short
legs.

3

Lizards Around the World

Lizards can be found worldwide, except at the North and South Poles. From Canada to Tierra del Fuego, lizards inhabit North and South America. Because lizards need the sun, there are more lizards closer to the *equator*.

In some regions, it stays warm even at night. Lizards like this Little Barking Gecko hunt at night to avoid the intense heat of the day.

In climates that are not as hot, such as the US, lizards are restricted to such sunny *habitats* as walls, sand dunes, outdoor walls, and riverbanks.

The Fringe-toed Lizard has special scales on its toes that allow it to run over loose sand.

The Lizard's Body

The design of the lizard's body is basically the same in all *species*. Lizards have a head, followed by the front legs, a long body, hind legs, and a tail that is three and sometimes four times the length of the body. Of course, not all lizards are exactly alike. Some are legless, and the skink has a round body and smooth scales for slithering through the undergrowth.

The head is the same for most lizards. They have nostrils that are used for breathing, but not smelling. They usually have good eyesight, with eyes on either side of their head. Their ears have a thin, almost *transparent* scale covering them for protection.

The lizard uses its tongue like a snake to "smell" the air. The lizard also has scaly skin, which it sheds occasionally to stay clean and rid itself of *parasites* such as ticks and mites.

The Lizard's Tail

The lizard's tail is important for many reasons. For lizards that live in trees most of the time, their tails help them balance. Some iguanas use their thick tails to help them swim through ocean waves.

Tails are used as weapons by some lizards. Monitor lizards from Africa, Asia, and Australia have long, whip-like tails, which they swing at enemies. The mastigure from the desert has spines on its tail.

Chameleons and some geckoes and skinks use their tail like a fifth leg. It is called a *prehensile* tail. The chameleon can hang from its tail like a monkey.

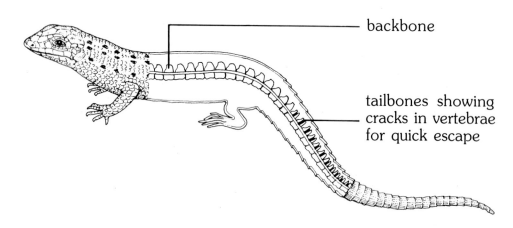

backbone

tailbones showing cracks in vertebrae for quick escape

The other, rather surprising way lizards can use their tail is by losing it. Lizards like this Green Day Gecko shed their tails and grow back new ones.

This ability is helpful when a *predator* gets hold of the tail. The lizard twists one of the cracked bones within the tail, the tail breaks off, and the lizard escapes. The tail continues to wriggle, so the predator eats it while the lizard runs away.

The Lizard's Eye

Generally, lizards have excellent eyesight. On top of many lizards' heads is a third eye, the *pineal eye*. It is smaller than the other eyes, and it is used only for measuring sunlight.

The most interesting lizard's eyes are those of the chameleon. Each eye can move independently of the other, and when they both point in the same direction the chameleon has *stereoscopic* vision.

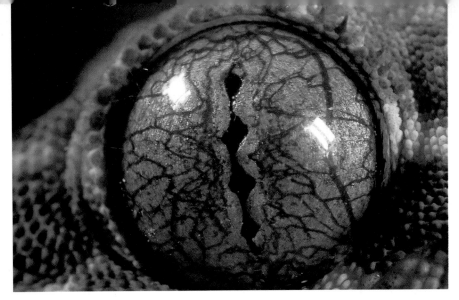

Geckoes are one of the few kinds of lizards that have no eyelids. Instead, the *pupil* closes while the gecko sleeps during the day and opens at night when it is active. The pupil controls how much sunlight goes into the gecko's eye.

There are some lizards that live underground all the time, and their eyesight has *degenerated*. They use their sense of smell to get around.

Movement

Lizards are fast runners, no matter how large or small they are. Chameleons have feet designed to grasp branches.

Basilisks can lift their front legs off the ground and run with "bipedal locomotion," like we do. Basilisks can run so fast this way, they can actually run across the surface of a river. This is why they are known to Central Americans as the "Jesus Christ" lizard.

The geckoes have the most fascinating feet of the lizards. On the underside of each of their five toes are hundreds of thousands of little hair-like scales. They allow the gecko to grip any surface, even smooth glass.

The Slow-worm is a lizard with no legs. It actually moves very fast and looks like a snake.

The Flying Lizard does not fly, but uses its flaps of skin to parachute to the ground.

Food and Feeding

Most lizards, like this gecko, are insectivorous.

Monitor lizards are both predators and *scavengers*. They will eat small mammals, and they will tear the flesh from dead animals with their sharp teeth. Monitors can reach 6-9 feet (2-3 m) in length.

Some species are herbivorous. The Marine Iguana, from the Galapagos Islands, feeds only on a certain seaweed it scrapes from underwater rocks.

Green Iguanas eat both plants and insects when they are small. But when they are older, they eat only leaves and fruit.

Some lizards specialize in only one kind of food. The Caiman Lizard of South America eats snails. The Australian Thorny Devil eats termites. Lizards either wait for their *prey* and then capture them, or they hunt them down. Like frogs, chameleons snap out their long, sticky tongues to catch insects.

Finding a Mate

The male lizard is more brightly colored than the female. He uses his bright colors both to attract a female during *courtship* and to drive off rival males from his area.

Male flying lizards of Southeast Asia have throat fans that they display upon landing on a new tree.

The male agamas have bright colors, while the females are dull brown.

Their coloring is an example of the *visual* signs lizards use for communicating. Only a few make any sounds at all.

Among the lizards that can make noises are the small house geckoes of Africa and Asia. They can be found on walls and ceilings making high-pitched clicking sounds.

Eggs

Most lizards, such as the Bearded Dragon, lay eggs in shallow holes in the ground and leave them to warm in the sun. Another way lizards reproduce is by keeping the eggs inside their bodies until just before they are ready to hatch.

For most, the eggs take several months before the *embryo* is developed enough to hatch. After about three months, the lizard hatches, head first.

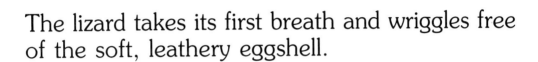

The lizard takes its first breath and wriggles free of the soft, leathery eggshell.

It hatches with a special "egg tooth" that it uses to crack the egg. After a few days, the lizard will shed its skin and the tooth.

The tiny lizard is a copy of its parents, already prepared to feed and fend for itself. It takes from a few months to a few years to grow to full size.

Live Young

If the lizard does not lay eggs, it carries the young inside a soft pouch until they hatch and emerge from the female's body.

By keeping the eggs inside her body, the female protects the eggs from such predators as small mammals, birds, insects, and other reptiles. This is one advantage to live birth.

The female can also be a mobile *incubator,* as she spreads herself out in the sun.

A disadvantage to live birth is that the mother is forced to carry the young inside her for up to three months, instead of using the time to lay more eggs. Also, she cannot always escape from predators.

This Shingleback Lizard from Australia (left) has given birth to two very large young. This newly-born Jackson's Chameleon (below) is one of a dozen born to its mother.

Enemies and Defense

When active, lizards use good sight and speed to avoid being caught. They hide under stones or in the ground when not active. In self-defense, lizards put on many displays. A Shingle-back Lizard opens its large pink mouth and shows its bright blue tongue in a harmless attempt to scare off a predator (above). This Australian Frilled Lizard (below) looks larger when it extends the flap of skin around its neck.

Many animals, including frogs, snakes (above), and even large spiders, prey on lizards. Some large species, such as South American iguanas, are even eaten by humans. This Green Iguana's head looks twice as big with a flap under its chin and an *eye-like* scale on its cheek.

Camouflage

A lizard's best way to avoid being eaten is not being seen at all. When an animal blends in with its background, it is *camouflaged*. This gecko can blend in perfectly with tree bark.

The anole lizards of South and North America can change their color from brown to green, depending on their background. Because of their skills in camouflage, they are sometimes called "American Chameleons."

True chameleons live in Southern Europe, Africa, and Asia. They have the ability to blend in with almost any color. Their secret is in their skin *cells*. The cells are filled with both dark and light particles, in different color-layers.

In order to make the camouflage work for them, lizards must move slowly. Chameleons can sway back and forth on a branch like a leaf blowing in the wind.

Lizards and People

Lizards that live in people's homes do a service by eating insects at night. Some lizards annoy people, however — like those that steal chickens and eggs. Others like to eat fruit out of tropical orchards. They are often shot or poisoned by the fruit growers.

False beliefs make lizards seem dangerous. It is believed in Trinidad that this Twenty-four Hours Lizard is deadly if you are bitten or touched by it. It is harmless.

Some species of lizard, like this Green Iguana from Central America, are hunted by humans for their skins and flesh.

There are only two known species of poisonous lizard: the Gila Monster and the Beaded Lizard. Both live in the southern United States. The most feared lizard is the Komodo Dragon, which is 12 feet long and eats goats and deer.

Friends and Neighbors

Thousands of insects, reptiles, birds, mammals, plants, and trees make up the tropical forest. Some of these animals are poisonous, such as this poison-arrow frog. Its bright colors are a warning.

Skinks, geckoes, and other lizards live side by side with — and feed upon — many insects under the logs and vegetation. The iguanas live high up in the trees, above tortoises, frogs, and crickets.

Many animals share the same food with lizards, too. Monkeys eat leaves, flowers, and fruit alongside the iguanas. Birds and bats will not harm the lizards. They feed on winged insects, such as this Clearwing Moth (above).

Living on the lizard's skin are tiny parasites. They are shed with the lizard's skin. And there are large insects, too, such as this huge millipede.

Life in the Jungle

There is always plenty of food and water for lizards in the jungle. The weather is always warm, and the soil is abundant for egg-laying. Their only problem in such a rich *environment* is the threat of predators.

Food Chain

Food chain

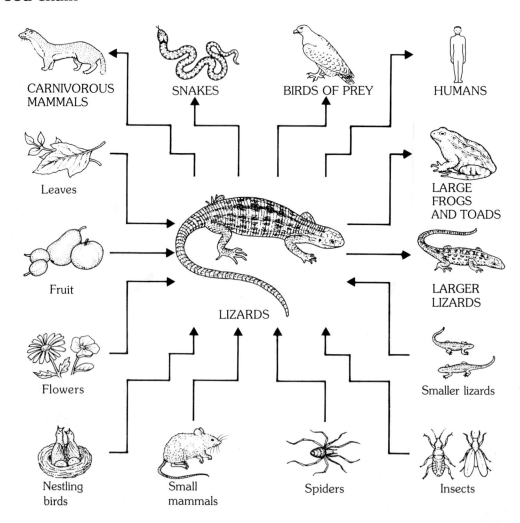

Lizards eat insects and are in turn eaten by large frogs and even spiders. The larger lizards are eaten by nocturnal mammals or snatched up by birds and snakes, as this food chain shows.

But the most serious threat to the lizard is people. Lizards and the animals who share the jungle with them are losing their habitat to the forest industry, and they can't last long on bare soil — especially if they are camouflaged to look like the bark of a tree or a dead leaf.

Index and New Words About Lizards

These new words about lizards appear in the text on the pages shown after each definition. Each new word first appears in the text in *italics*, just as it appears here.

Reading level analysis: FRY 4, FLESCH 85 (easy), RAYGOR 3.5, FOG 5, SMOG 3

Library of Congress Cataloging-in-Publication Data

Harrison, Virginia, 1966-
The world of lizards.

(Where animals live)
Adaptation of: The lizard in the jungle.
Includes index.
Text and photographs depict the characteristics, habits, and behavior of lizards around the world.
1. Lizards—Juvenile literature. [1. Lizards] I. Linley, Mike. Lizard in the jungle. II. Oxford Scientific Films. III. Title. IV. Series.
QL666.L2H33   1988   597.95   87-42608
ISBN 1-55532-332-4
ISBN 1-55532-307-3 (lib. bdg.)

North American edition first published in 1988 by Gareth Stevens Children's Books, 1555 North RiverCenter Drive, Suite 201, Milwaukee, Wisconsin 53212, USA. U.S. edition, this format, copyright © 1988 by Belitha Press Ltd. Text copyright © 1988 by Gareth Stevens, Inc. All rights reserved. No part of this book may be reproduced in any form or by any means without permission in writing from Gareth Stevens, Inc. First conceived, designed, and produced by Belitha Press Ltd., London, as **The Lizard in the Jungle**, with an original text copyright by Oxford Scientific Films. Format copyright by Belitha Press Ltd. Series Editor: Mark J. Sachner. Art Director: Treld Bicknell. Design: Naomi Games. Cover Design: Gary Moseley. Line Drawings: Lorna Turpin. Scientific Consultant: Gwynne Vevers.

The publishers wish to thank the following for permission to reproduce copyrighted material: **Oxford Scientific Films Ltd.** for pp. 7 both, 9, 15 above, 18 all, 19 all, 20, 24 below, 28, 29 both, and 31 (Mike Linley); title page (P. J. Devries); pp. 2, 11 above, 22 above, and 26 below (J. A. L. Cooke); pp. 3, 5, 6 both, 16, 22 below, 23 above, front cover, and back cover (Michael Fogden); pp. 4 and 17 (Anthony Bannister); p. 10 (Stephen Dalton); pp. 11 below and 27 (G. I. Bernard); pp. 12 and 14 (P. and W. Ward); p. 13 above (Breck P. Kent); pp. 13 below, 21, and 25 (Z. Lezczynski); p. 15 below (Godfrey Merlin); p. 23 below (Stuart Bebb); p. 24 above (Mantis Wildlife Films); p. 26 above (Peter Parks).

Printed in the United States of America
3 4 5 6 7 8 9 96 95 94 93 92 91

For a free color catalog describing Gareth Stevens' list of high-quality children's books, call 1-800-341-3569 (USA) or 1-800-461-9120 (Canada).